MW01482698

This Notebook Belongs To

Manufactured by Amazon.ca
Acheson, AB

31753708R00068